S0-ARC-918

■SCHOLASTIC

Shoe Box Learning Centers

Phonics

by Joan Novelli

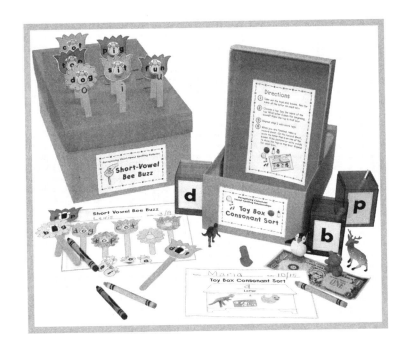

NEW YORK • TORONTO • LONDON • AUCKLAND • SYDNEY
MEXICO CITY • NEW DELHI • HONG KONG • BUENOS AIRES

Teaching *Resources*

Scholastic Inc. grants teachers permission to photocopy the activity sheets from this book for classroom use.
No other part of this publication may be reproduced in whole or in part, or stored in a retrieval system, or transmitted in any form
or by any means, electronic, mechanical, photocopying, recording, or otherwise, without written permission of the publisher.
For information regarding permission, write to Scholastic Inc., 557 Broadway, New York, NY 10012.

Cover design and photograph by Brian LaRossa
Interior design by Holly Grundon
Interior illustrations by James Graham Hale

ISBN 978-0-545-46869-5

Text copyright © 2012, 2006 by Joan Novelli.
Illustrations copyright © 2006 by Scholastic Inc.
Published by Scholastic Inc.
All rights reserved.
Printed in the U.S.A.

1 2 3 4 5 6 7 8 9 10   40   19 18 17 16 15 14 13 12

CONTENTS

About This Book

want to learn… When invited to complete this sentence at the beginning of kindergarten, my son's response came quickly: "I want to learn how to read." As with many young children, learning what to make of those symbols on a page was his quest, and once conquered, paved the way to an insatiable love of reading. A book (along with a basketball) goes with him almost everywhere.

What part does phonics play in helping children grow as independent readers? According to "The Role of Phonics in Reading Instruction," a position statement of the International Reading Association (IRA), "…there is a nearly unanimous regard for its importance." When combined with other knowledge of language (such as syntactic and contextual clues), the illustrations and print on a page, and children's own experiences and background knowledge, phonics instruction supports children in becoming successful readers.

Phonics instruction focuses on the relationship between sounds and symbols. As children learn to apply their knowledge of sound-symbol relationships, they enjoy increased and improved word recognition. Of course, one of the most compelling reasons to include phonics instruction in a reading and language arts program is that the less children struggle with word recognition, the more fluent they become, leaving more energy for content. This, in turn, helps improve comprehension and allows children to discover the magic in reading, which opens endless doors in school and beyond.

Shoe Box Learning Centers: Phonics makes it easy to create 30 engaging, portable centers that help children learn to read through hands-on exploration of sound-spelling relationships—including vowels, consonants, phonograms, final *e* spelling patterns, prefixes, suffixes, homophones, compound words, and syllabication. Each center fits neatly inside a shoe box and can be pulled out as needed and stored conveniently when not in use. Most shoe box centers are open-ended, which allows children to repeat the activity several times in the course of center time, building skills each time. When included as part of a reading program that provides direct instruction in phonics and offers plenty of opportunities for application, these centers can help children strengthen the skills they need to become fluent readers.

Setting Up Shoe Box Learning Centers

The games and activities in *Shoe Box Learning Centers: Phonics* are designed to be used by individual students and small groups of two to four students, but can easily be adapted for whole-class lessons or one-on-one teaching. Each center includes the following:

- **Label and Directions:** The title of each shoe box center becomes the shoe box label—simply glue it to one side (or end) of the shoe box for easy storage and retrieval. Cut out the student directions and glue to the inside lid of the shoe box.

- **Materials:** Check here to find out which items you'll need for each center.

- **Shoe Box Setup:** Here's where you'll find simple directions for assembling each center. In most cases, all you'll need to do is gather materials and make copies of the reproducibles.

- **Tips:** These helpful hints include ways to vary and extend the activities.

- **Reproducible Pages:** Record sheets, math mats, game boards, and patterns are just some of the shoe box center supplies included in the book.

To assemble the centers, photocopy each page on colored paper (or have children decorate), and cut out the title and directions along the lines as indicated. Glue the title to the outside of the box (on the end or side that will show when you stack and store the shoe boxes) and the directions to the inside of the lid. Assemble and prepare any other necessary materials (such as the reproducible activity pages), and place them in the box. You may want to enlist the help of parent volunteers or students to assist with this process.

Teaching With the Centers

This book is organized by skill areas, beginning with consonant sounds and the letters that represent them, followed by consonants and vowels in combination (such as CVC spelling patterns), more complex spelling patterns (digraphs, clusters, and phonograms), words that end in final *e*, prefixes, suffixes, plurals, and syllables. Word-building and writing skills are built into the centers, with record sheets provided for many centers.

The sequence in which you choose to teach with the centers may differ from the order of presentation in the book, depending on what best supports your reading program and your students' needs. Center activities are designed to be easily adapted to new phonics skills. For example, Toy Box Consonant Sort (page 9) focuses on initial consonant sounds. To broaden this focus and provide a challenge, include toys (or other objects) that have names beginning with consonant clusters (such as *bl*, *cl*, *fl*, and *tr*) and digraphs (such as *sh*, *ch*, and *th*). If you find that you want to provide more practice for a particular phonics skill, consider adapting a favorite center to provide a new phonics focus. This is easily done in many cases

To help students get the most out of using the centers, model the activities before inviting children to do them on their own.

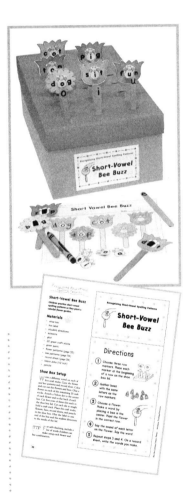

TIP

Many of the shoe box learning centers are easily adaptable for use with more than one phonics skill. Use correction fluid to change letters on manipulatives and patterns as desired and modify directions as needed. For example, with Short-Vowel Snowmen (page 24), children put together foam balls to make snowmen that spell CVC words, such as *cat*. To reinforce consonant digraphs (initial or final) with this shoe box center, write digraphs on either the smallest or largest ball (so that children can make words such as *ship* or *fish*).

simply by substituting one set of letters for another. For example, Compound Word Birds (page 57) provides practice in building and reading compound words. To focus on prefixes, just create a new set of cards that includes both prefixes and words they go with.

Reinforcing and Assessing Student Learning

One of the greatest benefits of using centers to strengthen reading skills is that they provide teachers with the opportunity to work with small groups or individuals on the concepts and skills being taught as part of the classroom reading program. The center setup makes it easy to review concepts and provide individual assistance as needed. To record students' progress as they move through centers, you may want to create assessment files. To do so, provide a pocket folder for each student. In the first pocket, place a checklist of all the centers so that students can keep track of those they have completed. (See page 7 for a reproducible Shoe Box Learning Centers Checklist.) In the second, have students store completed record sheets for you to review.

For activities that do not require record sheets, sticky notes work well as an assessment tool. Observe and talk with students as they work with a shoe box center. Jot comments on sticky notes, and record the child's name, the date, and the shoe box center name. Keep these on a separate sheet of paper in the pocket folder for easy reference. Comments for any center can be recorded on the checklist. Use these assessments to guide students' work with the centers. Encourage them to revisit centers where they show a need for more practice.

Meeting the Common Core State Standards

The center activities in this book will help you meet your specific state language arts standards as well as those recommended by the Common Core State Standards Initiative (CCSSI). The activities support students in meeting standards listed as Foundational Skills for Reading in the CCSSI documents. Students in grades K–2 are expected to demonstrate increasing awareness and competence in the areas that follow. For more details on these standards, go to the CCSSI Web site: www.corestandards.org.

Phonological Awareness
Demonstrate understanding of spoken words, syllables, and sounds (phonemes).

> RF.K.2a, RF.K.2b, RF.K.2c, RF.K.2d, RF.K.2e
> RF.1.2a, RF.1.2b, RF.1.2c, RF.1.2d

Phonics and Word Recognition
Know and apply grade-level phonics and word analysis skills in decoding words.

> RF.K.3a, RF.K.3b, RF.K.3d
> RF.1.3a, RF.1.3b, RF.1.3c, RF.1.3d, RF.1.3e, RF.1.3f, RF.1.3g
> RF.2.3a, RF.2.3b, RF.2.3c, RF.2.3d, RF.2.3e, RF.2.3f

To match specific skills and shoe box centers, see the skills matrix on page 8.

Shoe Box Learning Centers Checklist

Name_____

Shoe Box Learning Center	Date	Comments
Toy Box Consonant Sort		
Letters for Lunch		
Star, Star, Moon		
Recipe Box Reading		
Shopping for Words		
Magic Wand Words		
Telephone Phonics		
Button Up With Words		
Short-Vowel Snowmen		
Milk Jug Cap Stick-Ons		
Consonant Car Carrier		
Short-Vowel Bee Buzz		
Kangaroo Pocket Rhymes		
Nursery Rhyme Spelling		
Doggie, Doggie, Where's Your Bone?		
How Many Humps?		
Shoot for the Hoop!		
Talking Vowels		
The Great Erase		
Cereal Box Spellers		
Compound Word Birds		
Undo, Redo		
The End!		
Mystery Box Plurals		
Who's Got the Homophone?		
Snapshot Syllable Sort		
Bubble, Bubble		
Letter Olympics		
Scoop Shop Spelling		
Spot It, Say It, Spell It		

Phonics Skills Matrix

Shoe Box Learning Center	Consonants	Consonant Digraphs	Consonant Clusters	Short Vowels	Long Vowels	Vowel Digraphs	Final e	Structural Analysis	Vocabulary Development
Toy Box Consonant Sort	X			X					X
Letters for Lunch	X			X					X
Star, Star, Moon	X	X	X						X
Recipe Box Reading	X	X	X						X
Shopping for Words	X	X	X						X
Magic Wand Words	X			X					X
Telephone Phonics	X			X					X
Button Up With Words	X			X					X
Short-Vowel Snowmen	X			X					X
Milk Jug Cap Stick-Ons	X	X	X	X					X
Consonant Car Carrier	X	X	X	X					X
Short-Vowel Bee Buzz	X	X	X	X					X
Kangaroo Pocket Rhymes	X	X	X	X	X	X			X
Nursery Rhyme Spelling	X			X					X
Doggie, Doggie, Where's Your Bone?	X	X	X	X	X	X			X
How Many Humps?	X	X	X	X		X			X
Shoot for the Hoop!	X					X			X
Talking Vowels	X					X			X
The Great Erase	X			X	X		X		X
Cereal Box Spellers									X
Compound Word Birds	X	X	X	X	X	X	X	X	X
Undo, Redo								X	X
The End!								X	X
Mystery Box Plurals								X	X
Who's Got the Homophone?								X	X
Snapshot Syllable Sort	X			X				X	X
Bubble, Bubble								X	X
Letter Olympics	X	X	X	X	X	X	X	X	X
Scoop Shop Spelling	X	X	X	X	X	X	X	X	X
Spot It, Say It, Spell It	X	X	X	X	X	X	X	X	X

Toy Box Consonant Sort

Children sort toys into containers to match initial consonant sounds with letters.

Materials

- shoe box
- box label
- student directions
- scissors
- glue
- record sheet (page 10)
- toy boxes (small containers)
- small toys
- pencils
- crayons

Shoe Box Setup

Make copies of the toy box record sheets and cut apart. Write a consonant on each record sheet. Gather a collection of small toys with names that begin with these consonants in the initial position—for example:

B: ball, bear, balloon, bottle (toy baby bottle), bell, badge, bus

M: marble, magnet, mouse, monkey, mirror, motorcycle, mask

D: domino, duck, dish, dog, doll, dump truck, dollar (play money)

Label the toy boxes by consonant. Place the record sheets, toy boxes, toys, pencils, and crayons in the shoe box. Glue the label to one end of the box and the student directions to the inside of the lid.

TIP For a variation on this center, have children sort by consonant sounds in the final position or by vowel sounds.

Recognizing Consonant Sound-Spelling Relationships

Toy Box Consonant Sort

Directions

1 Take out the toys and boxes. Say the name of the letter on each box.

2 Choose a toy. Say the name of the toy. What letter makes the beginning sound? Place the toy in that box.

3 Repeat step 2 with more toys.

4 When you are finished, take a record sheet. On the record sheet, write the letter that is on one of the boxes. Draw pictures or write words to show the toys in that box. Repeat for each box.

Toy Box Consonant Sort

_____
Letter

Toy Box Consonant Sort

_____
Letter

Letters for Lunch

Children have fun with foods that match initial consonant sounds.

Materials

- shoe box
- box label
- student directions
- scissors
- glue
- paper plates (white)
- play food
- crayons

Shoe Box Setup

Write a consonant on each of several paper plates. Gather play foods (or glue pictures to index cards). You will need at least several foods that start with each consonant you use—for example:

B: bagel, butter, banana, beans, bacon, bok choy

C: carrot, cookie, cake, cucumber, corn, cauliflower

P: potato, pea, pancake, popcorn, pear, pita, pizza

S: sausage, sandwich, salad, soup, sushi

Place the plates, play food, and crayons in the shoe box. Glue the label to one end of the box and the student directions to the inside of the lid.

TIP Invite children to help stock this shoe box center with their favorite foods. They can cut out pictures and glue each one on a card. Use foods such as strawberries, spaghetti, broccoli, cherries, and peas to include consonant clusters and digraphs in this center.

Recognizing Consonant Sound-Spelling Relationships

Letters for Lunch

Directions

1. Choose a plate with a letter on it. Say the letter. Listen to the sound it makes.

2. Look for foods that start with that sound.

3. Place the foods on the plate.

4. Take a plain plate. Write the letter on the plate. Draw a picture of the foods you chose. Write your name.

Star, Star, Moon

Children stamp pictures to show what they know about letters and the sounds they make.

Materials

- shoe box
- box label
- student directions
- scissors
- glue
- picture strips (page 13)
- star and moon stamps (or any two different shapes or colors)

Shoe Box Setup

Make copies of the picture strips and cut them apart. Place the picture strips and stamps in the shoe box. Glue the label to one end of the box and the student directions to the inside of the lid.

TIP For a challenge, children can write the whole word beneath each picture, highlighting the initial consonants that have the same sound. For a variation, create picture strips to teach words with initial consonant digraphs and clusters (such as *clock, cloud, crayon*). Look for pictures in old magazines or workbooks.

Differentiating Between Beginning Consonant Sounds

Star, Star, Moon

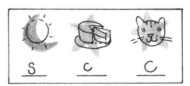

Directions

① Take a picture card. Say the name of each picture.

② Stamp a star on the pictures that have the same beginning sound.

③ Stamp a moon on the picture that does not have the same beginning sound.

④ On the blank line under the picture, write the letter that each word begins with.

⑤ Choose a new card. Repeat steps 1 through 4.

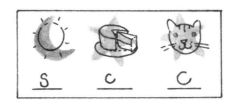

Star, Star, Moon

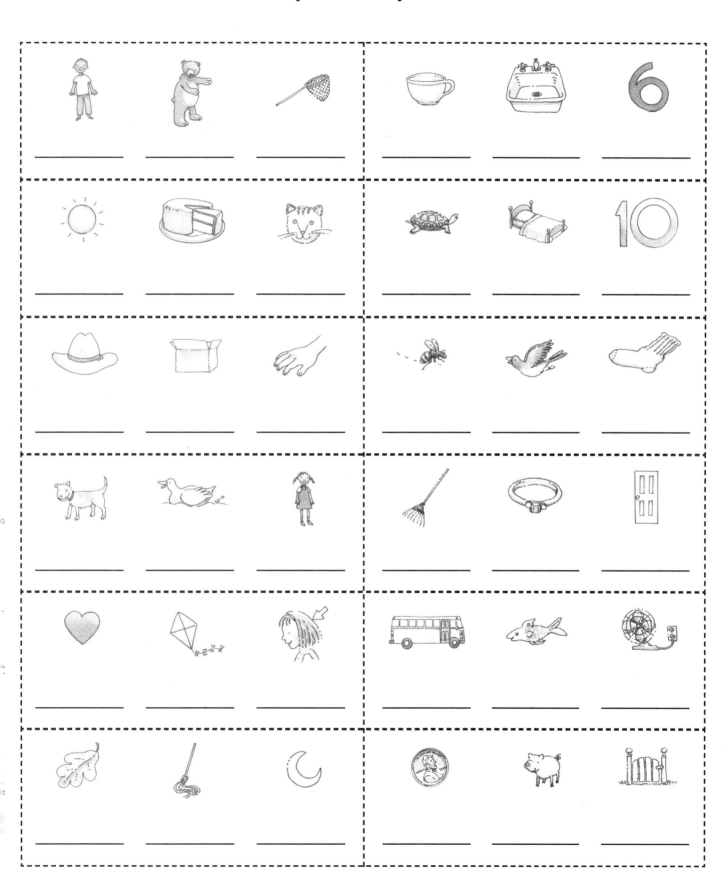

Recipe Box Reading

Children name and sort pictures of favorite foods to reinforce sound-spelling relationships.

Materials

- shoe box
- box label
- student directions
- scissors
- glue
- index cards
- pictures of foods
- recipe box with ABC dividers
- small blank books (see below)
- crayons
- pencils

Shoe Box Setup

Glue pictures of foods on index cards, one per card. Represent as many different letters as possible. Label each picture. Make blank books to provide opportunities for writing and to serve as a record of students' work. (Staple 27 half sheets of paper together. Write the name of the center on the cover.) Label each remaining page with a letter of the alphabet (in ABC order). Place the index cards, recipe box, books, crayons, and pencils in the shoe box. Glue the label to one end of the box and the student directions to the inside of the lid.

TIP This is a good center for partner work. Children can take turns choosing pictures and placing them behind the correct letter while their partners check the work.

Recognizing Sound-Letter Relationships

Recipe Box Reading

Directions

1 Open the recipe box. Say the letter on each card.

2 Choose a picture. Say the word for the picture. What letter does the word begin with?

3 Place the picture in the recipe box behind the matching letter.

4 Take out the pictures. Start with A. Read the word for each picture. Write it in your book.

Shopping for Words

Children roll game cubes to practice making sound-letter associations for beginnings and endings of words.

Materials

- shoe box
- box label
- student directions
- scissors
- glue
- game cube pattern and shopping list (page 16)
- pencils

Shoe Box Setup

Make 5 to 10 copies of the game cube. On one cube, write the numerals 1 though 6. On another cube, write the words "Begin" and "End" (three sides each). On the remaining cubes, paste small pictures of foods (such as from computer clip art) that children are likely to recognize. Aim for foods that represent a variety of beginning and ending sounds or letters, such as soup, popcorn, doughnut, chicken, bagel, and muffin. Make copies of the shopping list. Place the game cubes, shopping lists, and pencils in the shoe box. Glue the label to one end of the box and the student directions to the inside of the lid.

TIP **T**o simplify this game, repeat the numbers 1 and 2 on the number cube. As children become familiar with the foods on the picture cubes, make new ones. Stay with the food theme, or go with something new—for example, animals.

Recognizing Beginning and Ending Sounds

Shopping for Words

Directions
(for 2 players)

① Each player takes a shopping list and a pencil. Players take turns rolling three cubes: a picture cube, a Begin–End cube, and a number cube.

② The player says the name of the food. The Begin–End cube tells if the player is going to list foods that begin or end with the same sound as the picture rolled. The number cube tells how many items the player will list.

③ On a shopping list, players draw pictures or write words for the items they name.

Shopping for Words

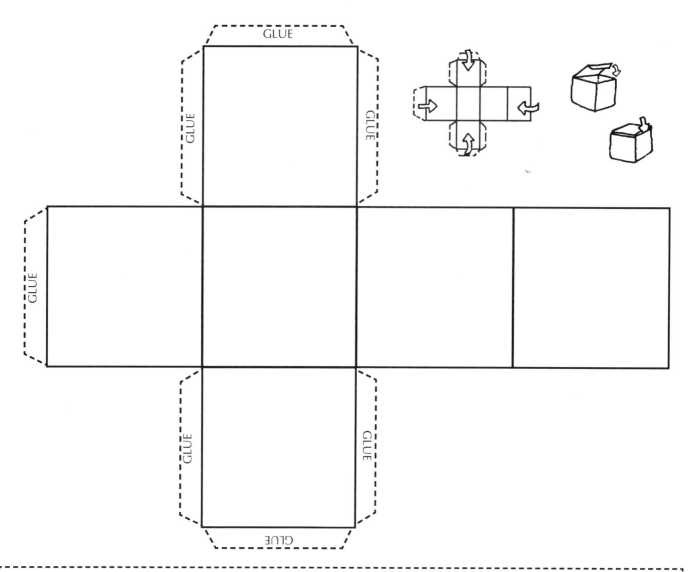

GLUE

GLUE

GLUE

GLUE

GLUE

GLUE

GLUE

_____'s
Shopping List

Magic Wand Words

A magic wand adds a special touch as children read and form words with magnetic letters.

Materials

- shoe box
- box label
- student directions
- scissors
- glue
- mini magic wand (see below)
- picture and word cards (page 18)
- snack-size resealable plastic bags
- magnetic letters
- covered plastic container

Shoe Box Setup

Make a mini magic wand by gluing a sparkly star to one end of an unsharpened pencil or a small dowel. Attach a few glittery ribbons. Copy the picture and word cards onto card stock and cut them apart. Place each pair (picture card and word card) in a resealable plastic bag. Place magnetic letters in a covered container. Place the wand, picture and word card sets, and magnetic letters in the shoe box. Glue the label to one end of the box and the student directions to the inside of the lid.

TIP **T**o simplify this activity, place the magnetic letters in a sorting tray (with a compartment for each letter). If this tray doesn't fit in the shoe box, place it at the center where children will be working.

Reading and Forming CVC Words

Magic Wand Words

Directions

① Choose a bag. Take out the picture card and word card. Say the word.

② Use the letters to make the word.

③ Read the word. Use the magic wand to point to each letter.

cat

dog

c a t

d o g

Magic Wand Words

cat	hat	dot	dog
pig	sun	bed	log
net	sad	ten	pen
pin	bug	bus	box

Telephone Phonics

Children dial numbers to see what words they can spell.

Materials

- shoe box
- box label
- student directions
- scissors
- glue
- telephone book (pages 20–21)
- toy telephone
- pencils

Shoe Box Setup

Make copies of the telephone book pages. Cut apart the pages for each telephone book and staple to bind. (You may include only those pages that best match students' ability, or put the entire book together but flag the pages you'd like them to complete.) Place the telephone books, telephone, and pencils in the shoe box. Glue the label to one end of the box and the student directions to the inside of the lid.

TIP **T**o simplify this activity, cover the numbers on the phone with small, round stickers. On each sticker, write the corresponding number and only one of the three letters. Choose those letters that will most easily make CVC words when combined with a vowel in the middle position. For example, you might use the *b* with the 2 keypad, *d* for 3, *h* for 4, *l* for 5, *m* for 6, *p* for 7, *t* for 8, and *y* for 9. For a more challenging game, use combinations of four letters and numbers to spell four-letter words.

Recognizing Initial and Final Consonants

Telephone Phonics

Directions

(1) Take a telephone book. Write your name on it.

(2) Choose a number to call.

(3) Look at the letters on the phone that go with each number. Choose one for each number to spell a word.

(4) Write the three letters in order in the spaces. Read the word.

(5) Repeat steps 2 through 4 to make new words.

Telephone Book

_____'s

Telephone Book

Telephone Number	Write the Word
4 o p	_____
9 i p	_____
5 a m	_____
3 u n	_____
c a 8	_____
d o 4	_____
m a 7	_____
r e 3	_____

1

2

20

Make up your own phone numbers.
Ask a friend to find the word.

Telephone Number	Write the Word
(consonant) (number) (consonant)	_____
(consonant) (number) (consonant)	_____
(consonant) (number) (consonant)	_____
(consonant) (number) (consonant)	_____
(consonant) (number) (consonant)	_____
(consonant) (number) (consonant)	_____

4

Telephone Number	Write the Word
2 e d	_____
7 e t	_____
7 u n	_____
2 o x	_____
4 o 8	_____
4 e 6	_____
2 u 7	_____
2 i 4	_____

3

Button Up With Words

Children "sew" missing buttons on jackets to practice spelling and reading CVC words.

Materials

- shoe box
- box label
- student directions
- scissors
- glue
- jacket patterns (page 23)
- dot stickers
- buttons (about 1/2 inch in diameter; at least 24)
- small container with cover

Shoe Box Setup

Make and cut out copies of the jacket patterns. Write a consonant on the top button of each jacket. Write consonants and vowels on dot stickers (one per sticker). Make at least two of each. Choose consonants that have a high frequency of use in CVC words, such as *s*, *t*, *m*, *f*, *r*, *b*, *l*, *c*, *h*, and *p*. Place a sticker on each button. Store the buttons in the container. Place the jackets and buttons in the shoe box. Glue the label to one end of the box and the student directions to the inside of the lid.

TIP As a variation, substitute consonant digraphs and blends in the first (or last) button position. For a challenge, make copies of the jacket patterns but do not fill in any letters. Have children choose three buttons for each jacket and place them in order to spell a word.

Recognizing CVC Spelling Patterns

Button Up With Words

Directions

(1) Choose a jacket. Color it.

(2) Read the letter on the button. Count the missing buttons.

(3) Find buttons that will spell a word on the jacket. Place them on the jacket in order.

(4) Read your word. Write it on a sheet of paper.

(5) Take off the buttons. Repeat steps 1 through 3 to make as many words as you can with your jacket.

(6) Choose a new jacket. Make more words.

Button Up
With Words

Button Up
With Words

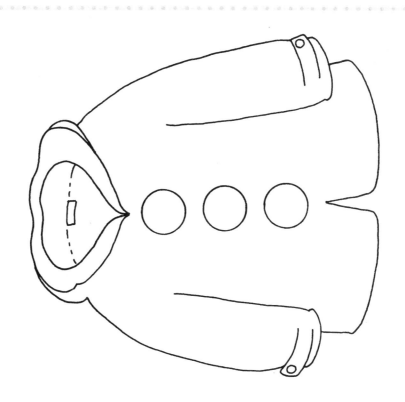

Short-Vowel Snowmen

Children build snowmen to practice making and reading words with short-vowel spelling patterns.

Materials

- shoe box
- box label
- student directions
- scissors
- glue
- foam balls (3 inch, 5 inch, 6 inch)
- record sheet (page 25)
- toothpicks
- pencils

Shoe Box Setup

Write consonants on the small and large foam balls (one letter per ball). Write vowels on the medium foam balls (one letter per ball). You may repeat consonants and vowels to provide multiple opportunities for using them to spell words. Make copies of the record sheet. Place the foam balls, record sheets, toothpicks, and pencils in the shoe box. Glue the label to one end of the box and the student directions to the inside of the lid.

TIP You may wish to teach continuous consonants first, including *f, l, m, n, r, s, v,* and *z.* Also consider the frequency of use when introducing consonants. For example, *s, t, m, f, r, b, l, c, h,* and *p* have a higher frequency of use than *k, v, z, x, y,* and *q.* For practice with consonant digraphs and blends, include these on both small and large balls (in initial and final position).

Practicing Short-Vowel Spelling Patterns

Short-Vowel Snowmen

Directions

(1) Sort the snowballs into three groups: small, medium, and large.

(2) Use three snowballs (one of each size) to spell a word. The first letter is the small snowball. The second letter is the medium snowball. The last letter is the large snowball.

(3) Use the toothpicks to stick the snowballs together.

(4) Write your word on the record sheet. Repeat, using more snowballs to make new words. Read your words.

 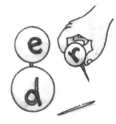 

Short-Vowel Snowmen

Name _____   Date _____

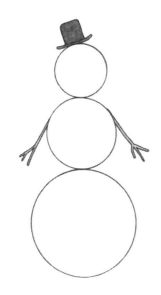 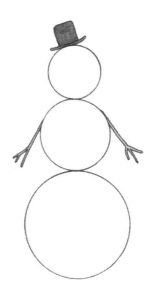 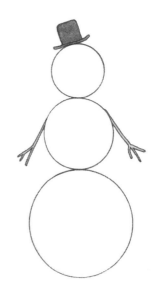

Short-Vowel Snowmen

Name _____   Date _____

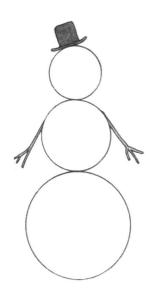 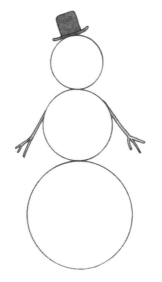 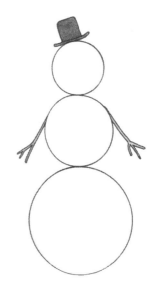

Milk Jug Cap Stick-Ons

Children use milk jug caps to make words in an activity that teaches consonant blend sound-spelling relationships.

Materials

- shoe box
- box label
- student directions
- scissors
- glue
- milk jug caps (at least 25)
- permanent marker
- Velcro
- record sheet (page 27)
- pencils

Shoe Box Setup

Write a letter or letters on the inside of each milk jug cap. Make at least two sets of vowels, 15 to 20 consonants, and the following consonant blends: *cl, fl, pl, sn, sl, st, dr, sp, tr, cr.* Number the caps on the reverse side as follows: 1 (consonant blends), 2 (vowels), and 3 (individual consonants). Glue pieces of Velcro to the shoe box to make four or five rows of three each. Space the Velcro to fit a cap in each spot. Glue a piece of Velcro to the top side of each cap. Make copies of the record sheet. Place the caps, record sheets, and pencils in the shoe box. Glue the label to one end of the box and the student directions to the inside of the lid.

TIP **T**o simplify this activity, set up the center in advance, placing vowels and final consonants in position. Have children use the consonant blend milk caps to complete each word.

Practicing Consonant Blend Spelling Patterns

Milk Jug Cap Stick-Ons

Directions

(1) Find milk jug caps with the letters *cl, a,* and *p.* Stick the milk jug caps on the shoe box in order. Write the word on the record sheet.

(2) Choose three new milk caps to make a word. Choose one for each number (1, 2, 3).

(3) Stick the milk caps on the shoe box in order to spell your word. Write the word on the record sheet.

(4) Make more words with the milk caps. Write them on the record sheet. Read your words.

Name _____

Date _____

Milk Jug Cap
Stick-Ons

Name _____

Date _____

Milk Jug Cap
Stick-Ons

Consonant Car Carrier

Children fill a car carrier with cars to practice matching consonant sounds, including consonant blends, with letters.

Materials

- shoe box
- box label
- student directions
- scissors
- glue
- record sheet (page 29)
- car carrier patterns (pages 30–31)
- small toy cars
- pencils
- crayons

Shoe Box Setup

Make copies of the record sheet. Copy the car carrier patterns onto card stock and glue or tape them together to form a complete truck. Write a consonant on each of the four spaces. Place the car carrier, record sheets, cars, pencils, and crayons in the shoe box. Glue the label to one end of the box and the student directions to the inside of the lid.

TIP To allow more than one child to work independently at this center, make multiple car carriers with different sets of consonants.

Practicing Consonant Sound-Letter Relationships

Consonant Car Carrier

Directions

(1) Take a car carrier. Look at a letter. Find a car that matches that letter. (The name or color of the car might start with the letter, or there may be another attribute of the car that matches.)

(2) Place the car on the letter.

(3) Repeat steps 1 and 2 to fill the car carrier. On a record sheet, draw and color each car. Write the letter.

Consonant Car Carrier

Name _____

Date _____

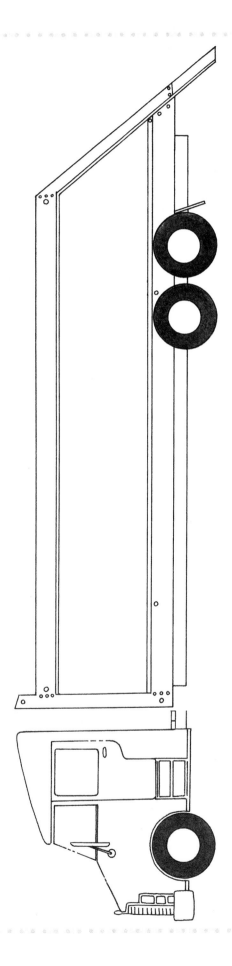

Consonant Car Carrier

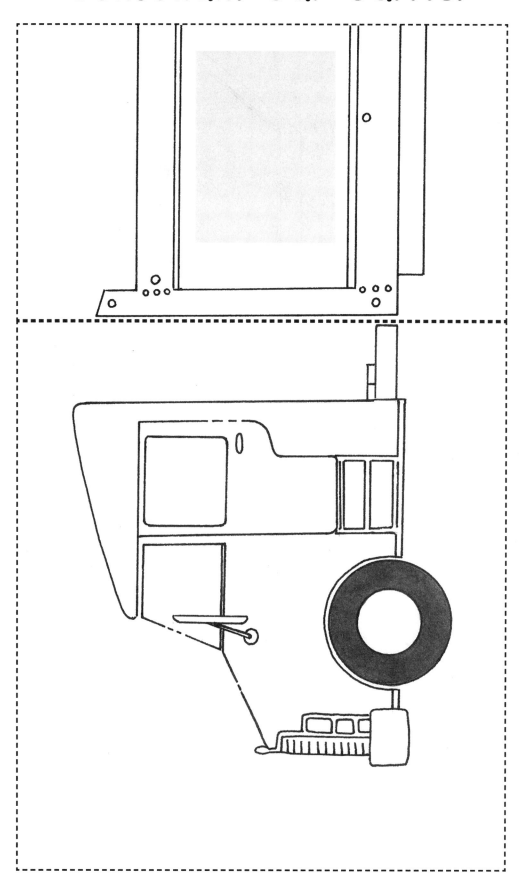

Consonant Car Carrier

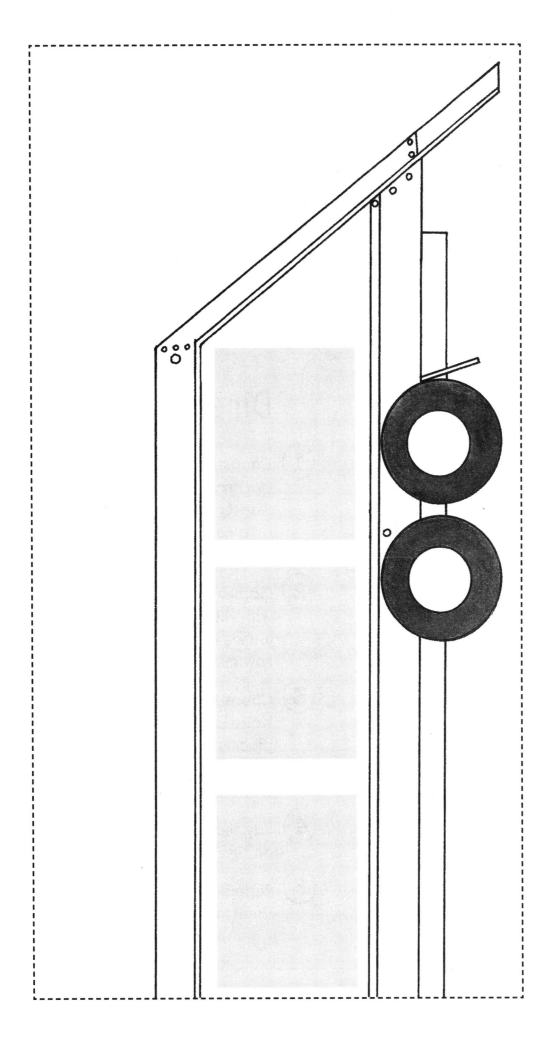

Short-Vowel Bee Buzz

Children practice short-vowel spelling patterns as they plant a colorful flower garden.

Materials

- shoe box
- box label
- student directions
- scissors
- glue
- 20 green craft sticks
- green paint
- flower patterns (page 33)
- bee patterns (page 34)
- record sheet (page 34)
- Velcro dots (1/2 inch)
- pencils

Shoe Box Setup

Write a different vowel on each of five craft sticks. Copy the flower and bee patterns and record sheet. Color and cut out the flowers and bees. Glue a flower to each of the remaining 20 craft sticks. Attach a Velcro dot to the center of each flower and to the back of each bee. Cut five rows of three slits each in the shoe box lid. Cut each slit to snugly hold a craft stick. Place the craft sticks, flowers, bees, record sheets, and pencils in the shoe box. Glue the label to one end of the box and the student directions to the inside of the lid.

TIP For self-checking, include a list of words children can make using each flower and bee combination.

Short-Vowel Bee Buzz

Directions

1. Choose three row markers. Place each marker at the beginning of a row on the shoe box lid.

2. Gather bees with the same letters as the row markers.

3. Choose a flower. Make a word by placing a bee in the center. Plant the flower in the correct row.

4. Say the sound of each letter on the flower. Say the word.

5. Repeat steps 3 and 4. On a record sheet, write the words you make.

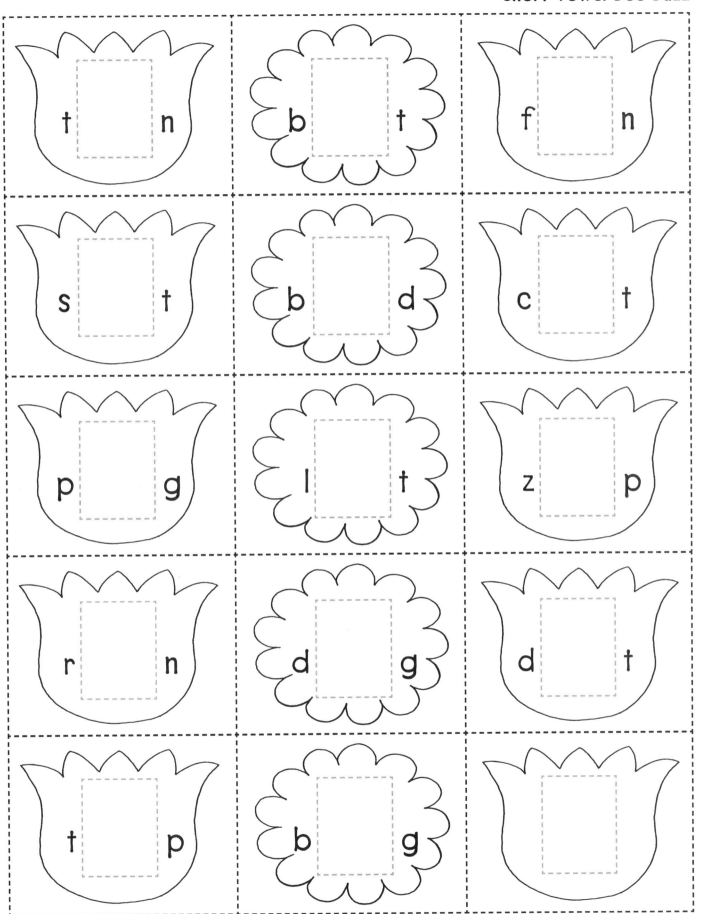

Short-Vowel Bee Buzz

Name_____ Date _____

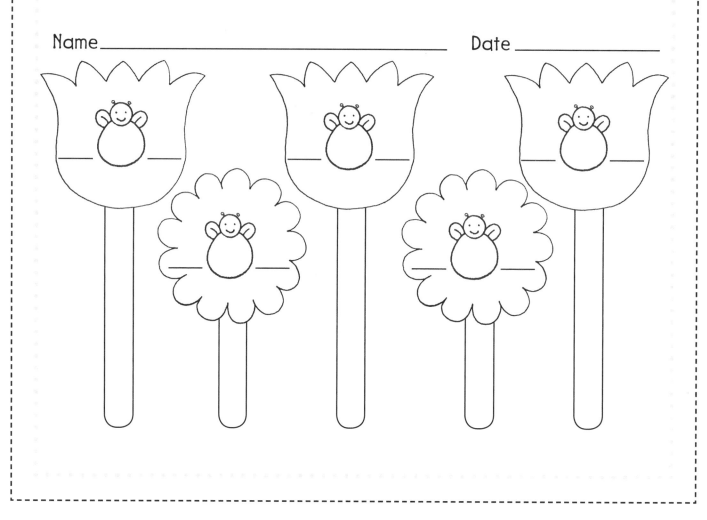

Kangaroo Pocket Rhymes

Children practice vowel-sound spelling patterns as they sort rhyming words into pockets.

Materials

- shoe box
- box label
- student directions
- scissors
- glue
- kangaroo and pocket patterns (page 36)
- joey cards (pages 37–38)

Shoe Box Setup

Copy the kangaroo and pocket pattern for each phonogram you want to include in the shoe box. Write phonograms you want to teach on the pocket patterns, one per pocket. Laminate each piece for durability. (The following phonograms are represented on the joey cards: -ump, -at, -ot, -ide, -ed, -eep, -ake, -ug, -all, -oom.) Glue or tape the side and bottom edges of each pocket to a kangaroo. Copy the joey cards. Laminate and cut apart the cards. Place the kangaroos and joey cards inside the shoe box. Glue the label to one end of the box and the student directions to the inside of the lid.

TIP Introduce this center with a look at ways kangaroos and other animals keep their babies safe. Written in rhyme (like the center's word cards), *Safe, Warm, and Snug*, by Stephen R. Swinburne (Gulliver Books, 1999), introduces marsupial, insect, bird, mammal, and reptile parents and babies.

Building Fluency With Phonograms

Kangaroo Pocket Rhymes

Directions

① Choose a kangaroo.

② Read the letters on the pocket. Say the sound the letters make.

③ Find a joey with a word that rhymes. Say the word. Jump the joey into the pocket.

④ Repeat step 3 for each joey that has a rhyming word.

⑤ Choose a new kangaroo and repeat.

Kangaroo Pocket Rhymes

Kangaroo Pocket Rhymes

jump   bump   pump   thump

bat   cat   pat   splat

hot   not   got   spot

hide   wide   ride   slide

bed   fed   red   sled

Kangaroo Pocket Rhymes

beep	deep	peep	sleep
bake	cake	lake	snake
dug	hug	tug	snug
ball	call	fall	small
boom	room	zoom	bloom

Nursery Rhyme Spelling

Children supply missing phonograms to complete nursery rhymes.

Materials

- shoe box
- box label
- student directions
- scissors
- glue
- sentence strips
- colorful clips
- lima beans
- permanent marker
- covered plastic container

Shoe Box Setup

Write familiar nursery rhymes on sentence strips, one line per strip. Leave blanks (one per letter) for the phonogram in one of two words that make a rhyming pair. Do this for each pair of rhyming words. Number the back of the sentence strips to indicate the correct order. Clip each set of sentence strips together. Write letters on lima beans that children can use to fill in the missing letters. (Make multiples of each letter so that children can leave them in place to complete the entire nursery rhyme.) Place the lima beans in a container. Place the nursery rhymes and lima beans in the shoe box. Glue the label to one end of the box and the student directions to the inside of the lid.

TIP As a variation, use the same format to focus on other phonics skills, such as initial and final consonants (including digraphs and clusters) and vowels.

Recognizing Word Family Spelling Patterns

Nursery Rhyme Spelling

Jack and Jill
went up the h _ _ _

Directions

(1) Choose a nursery rhyme.

(2) Place the sentence strips in order. Use the first word on each sentence strip to help. Or look at the numbers on the back.

(3) Take out the lima beans. Read the nursery rhyme. Use the lima beans to fill in the blanks with the missing letters. Read your nursery rhyme to a friend.

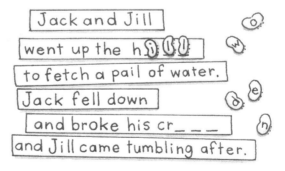

Doggie, Doggie, Where's Your Bone?

Children sort words into word families as they help dogs find their bones.

Materials

- shoe box
- box label
- student directions
- scissors
- glue
- dog patterns (page 41)
- large index cards
- bone patterns (page 42)
- resealable plastic bags
- sand
- record sheets (see Tip)
- pencils

Shoe Box Setup

Enlarge and copy the dog patterns. Color and cut them out, then glue to large index cards. Place each dog in a bag and label with the dog's name. Copy the bone patterns onto card stock and laminate. Cut out the bones, then cut each bone in two parts as indicated. Use the blank dog and bone cards to add a new phonogram. Pour about two inches of sand in the shoe box. Bury the bones in the sand. Place the dogs, record sheets, and pencils in the box. Glue the label to one end of the box and the student directions to the inside of the lid.

TIP To create record sheets, make extra copies of the dog patterns. Glue to lined paper and label. As children dig bones and put them together to make words, have them record the words on the matching record sheet.

Using Word Family Spelling Patterns

Doggie, Doggie, Where's Your Bone?

Directions

1. Choose a dog. Say the dog's name.

2. Help your dog find some bones. Dig in the sand. Try to put the bones together to make words that rhyme with your dog's name. Set the other bones to the side.

3. Write the words you make on the matching record sheet.

4. Choose a new dog. Repeat steps 2 and 3.

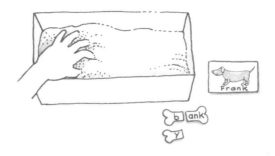

Doggie, Doggie, Where's Your Bone?

Spot

Queen

King

Jack

Frank

Doggie, Doggie, Where's Your Bone?

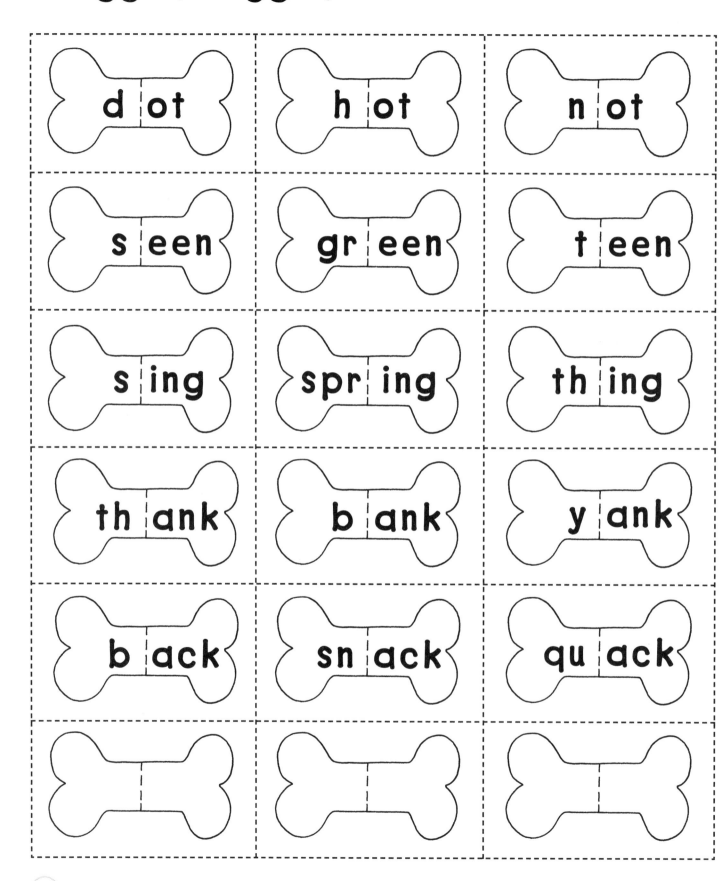

d ot

h ot

n ot

s een

gr een

t een

s ing

spr ing

th ing

th ank

b ank

y ank

b ack

sn ack

qu ack

How Many Humps?

Children help camels find their humps to practice spelling with vowel pairs.

Materials

* shoe box
* box label
* student directions
* scissors
* glue
* camel pattern (page 44)
* resealable plastic bag
* paper
* pencils
* crayons

Shoe Box Setup

Make multiple copies of the camel pattern on card stock and cut apart. Give each camel a name that represents a vowel diagraph. Suggestions: Keely (*ee*), Cooper (*oo*), Shawn (*aw*), Jean (*ea*), Jaiden (*ai*), Moira (*oi*). Write the camel name on the camel and the vowel digraph on the hump. Place the separate camel humps in a bag. Place the camel patterns, humps, paper, pencils, and crayons in the shoe box. Glue the label to one end of the box and the student directions to the inside of the lid.

TIP Use the blank camel hump patterns to add new letters for children to work with. Include consonant digraphs and clusters for children to use in either the initial or final position.

Practicing Vowel Digraph Spelling Patterns

How Many Humps?

Directions

1. Choose a camel. Say the camel's name.

2. This camel has one hump. Give it more! Place one or more humps on the camel to spell a word.

3. Say the word. Write the word on a sheet of paper.

4. Give your camel new humps to make new words. Write the words.

How Many Humps?

b	w	h	l	p	oi	ai
c	f	s	m	t	oo	ea
d	g	j	n	r	ee	aw

Shoot for the Hoop!

Children sharpen vowel spelling patterns in this race to the hoop.

Materials

- shoe box
- box label
- student directions
- scissors
- glue
- game cards and markers (pages 46–47)
- game board (pages 48–49)
- crayons

Shoe Box Setup

Copy the game cards and game markers onto card stock and cut them apart. Copy the game board onto card stock. Glue the two sides together at the center. Color the game markers different colors if desired. Place the cards, game board, and game markers in the shoe box. Glue the label to one end of the box and the student directions to the inside of the lid.

TIP The vowel digraph *oo* has two sounds: a long /o͞o/ (as in *hoop* and *school*) and a short /o͝o/ (as in *book* and *full*). The long sound occurs more often and with more spellings than the short sound. One helpful strategy for children to learn is to try the long sound first to see if the resulting word sounds familiar.

Differentiating Spelling Patterns for Variant Vowels

Shoot for the Hoop!

Directions
(for 2 or more players)

1. Each player takes a marker. Shuffle the cards. Place them facedown next to the game board.

2. The first player chooses a card and reads the word.

3. If the word has the same vowel sound as *hoop*, the player gets a basket and moves ahead two spaces. If the word does not have the same vowel sound as *hoop*, the player does not move. Every player must get a word with the same vowel sound as *hoop* to move off Start. Players follow directions on spaces they land on.

4. Players take turns until one player makes it to the hoop on the board.

Shoot for the Hoop!

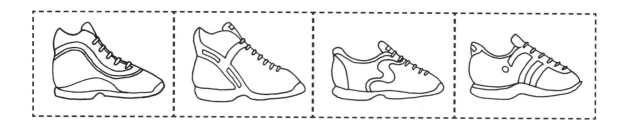

ball	store	too	do
boom	group	good	hop
zoom	toy	cook	stop
hoop	chew	zoo	cool
shoot	flew	shoo	pool
few	boo	goof	tool
blew	moo	roof	school

Shoot for the Hoop!

tooth	tube	took	spot
hoot	dude	foot	box
toot	blue	wood	more
scoop	glue	full	loud
hour	true	push	cow
loop	sure	door	shout
spoon	tune	floor	down
moon	frog	roar	clown
soup	book	fork	mouse

Shoot for the Hoop!

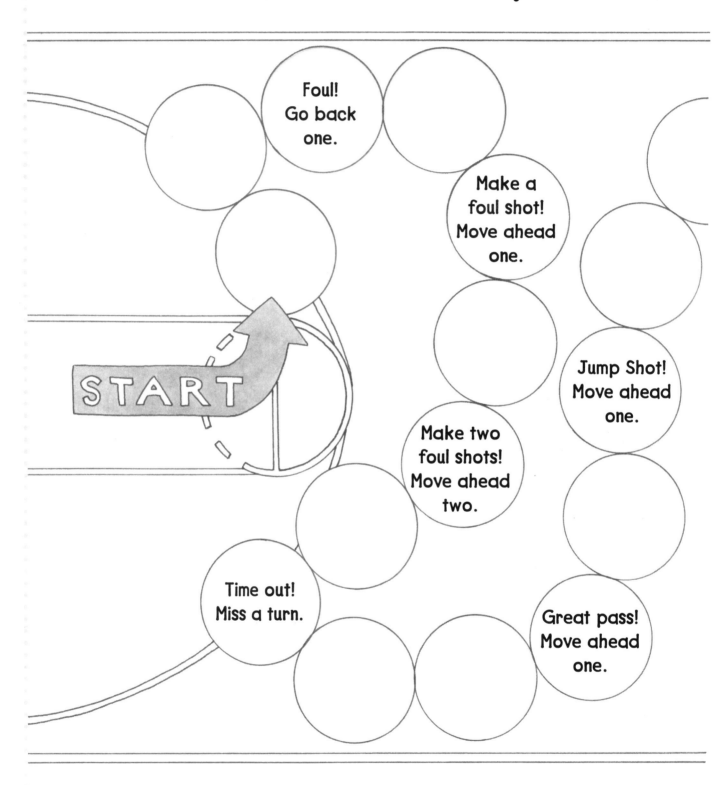

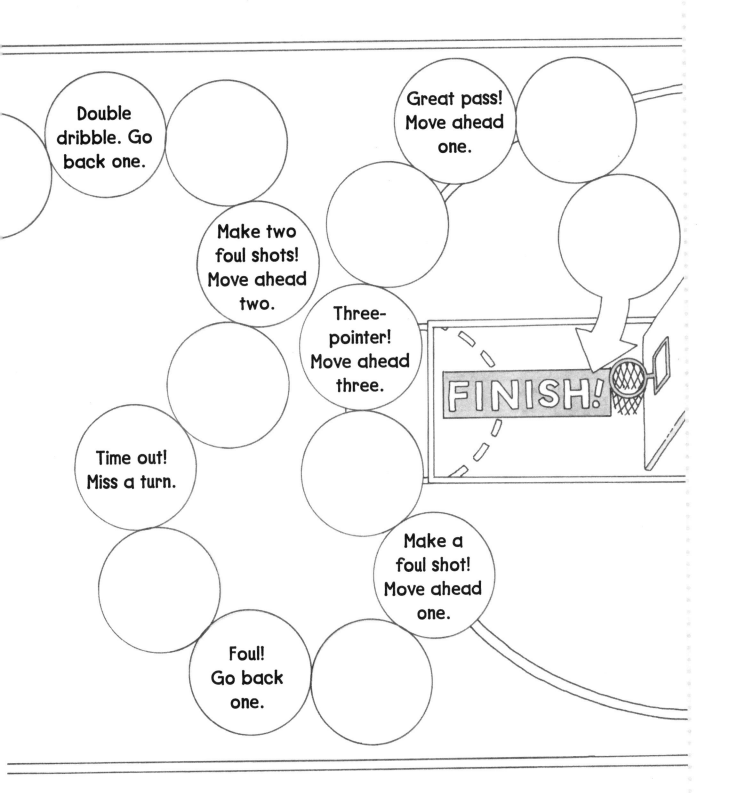

Talking Vowels

Children match vowel digraphs with the same sound but different spellings while being introduced to writing dialogue.

Materials

* shoe box
* box label
* student directions
* scissors
* glue
* picture cards (pages 51–52)
* word cards (page 52)
* puff paint

Shoe Box Setup

Copy the picture cards onto card stock. Copy the word cards onto card stock and cut them apart. Use puff paint to outline each speech bubble. Place the picture cards and word cards in the shoe box. Glue the label to one end of the box and the student directions to the inside of the lid.

TIP Add to this center by making new picture and word cards for other vowel digraphs. This center is also easily adapted to teach other phonics skills, such as initial letters ("I begin with the same letter as _____," said the _____.) and rhyming words ("I rhyme with ___," said the _____.).

Practicing Vowel Digraph Spelling Patterns

Talking Vowels

Directions

① Choose a picture card.

② Read the sentence.

③ Find the word card that goes in the blank. Place the word card in the sentence. Read the sentence again.

Talking Vowels

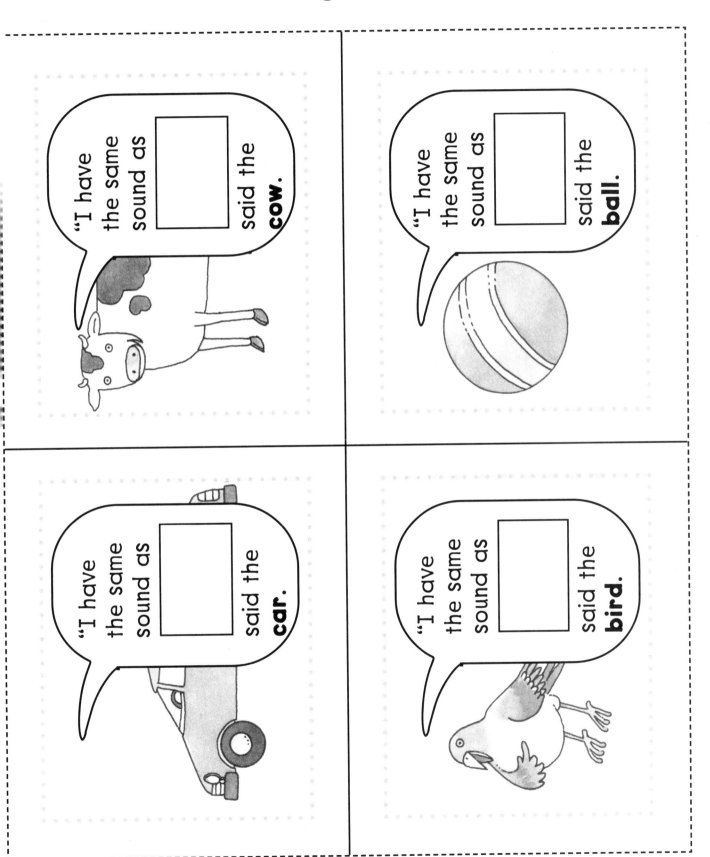

"I have the same sound as ☐ said the **cow.**

"I have the same sound as ☐ said the **ball.**

"I have the same sound as ☐ said the **car.**

"I have the same sound as ☐ said the **bird.**

Talking Vowels

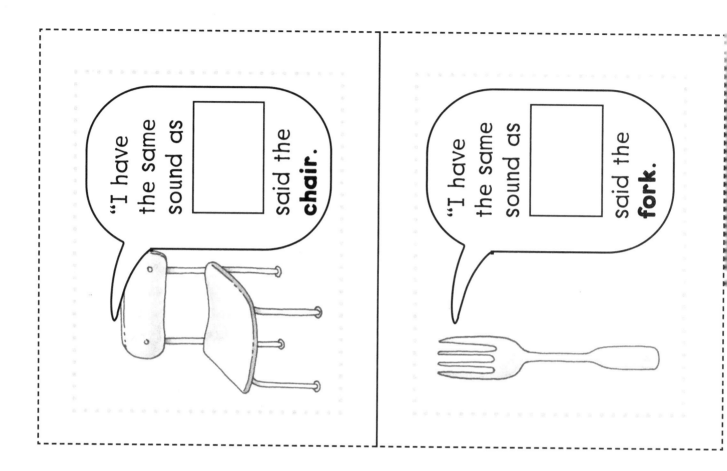

The Great Erase

Children investigate words with the silent (final) e spelling pattern.

Materials

- shoe box
- box label
- student directions
- scissors
- glue
- word lists (page 54)
- small white board
- dry-erase marker
- small white board eraser

Shoe Box Setup

C opy and cut apart the word lists. Place the word lists, white board, marker, and eraser in the shoe box. Glue the label to one end of the box and the student directions to the inside of the lid.

TIP **F** or practice making and reading the original words, children can add the final e back to the words once they've read the list of new words. This will reinforce the CVCe spelling pattern. To go further, introduce other regular spelling patterns for final e— for example, CCVCe (*whale*), CCCVCe (*stripe*), and VCe (*ate*).

Exploring Final e Spelling Patterns

The Great Erase

Directions
(for 2 players)

1 One player chooses a word list. This player copies the words onto the white board.

2 The other player takes the white board and eraser.

3 The player with the word list reads a word. The player with the white board finds the word and reads it. This player erases the final e.

4 Repeat step 3 for all words on the list.

5 Together, players read the new words without the final e. Then they find the one that is not a real word and circle it.

6 Players change places and play with a new word list.

The Great Erase

Word List

- tape
- bite
- hope
- cute
- cake

Word List

- joke
- made
- ripe
- ride
- cane

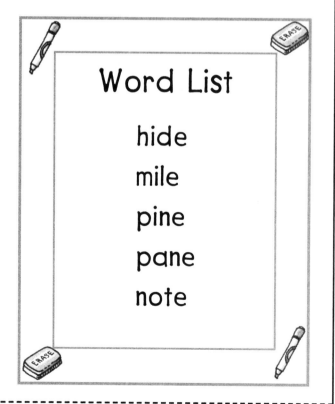

Word List

- hide
- mile
- pine
- pane
- note

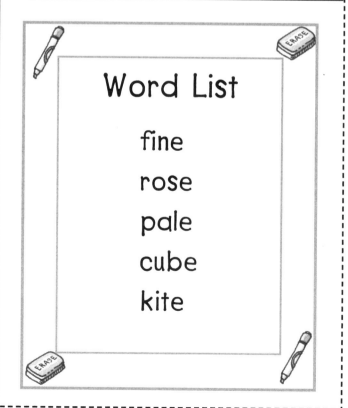

Word List

- fine
- rose
- pale
- cube
- kite

Cereal Box Spellers

Children build sight-word vocabulary with a favorite food—cereal!

Materials

- shoe box
- box label
- student directions
- scissors
- glue
- single-serving cereal boxes
- high-frequency word tiles (page 56)
- tagboard
- resealable plastic bag
- markers
- crayons

Shoe Box Setup

Copy and laminate the word tiles. (Use the blanks to add words.) Cut apart the tiles and place them in a resealable plastic bag. Cut tagboard pieces that are the same size as the cereal boxes. Place the word tiles, tagboard, markers, and crayons in the shoe box. Glue the label to one end of the box and the student directions to the inside of the lid.

TIP Learning high-frequency words, many of which have irregular spellings, is important to reading fluency. To help children build a strong sight-word vocabulary, review these words periodically. Let children practice writing the letters in different ways (tracing them, writing them in the air, forming them with clay strips, and so on) as they spell and say them.

Recognizing Sound-Letter Relationships in High-Frequency Words

Cereal Box Spellers

Directions

1. Choose a cereal box. Look at the words on the cereal box. Find word tiles that match.

2. Place the word tiles on top of the matching words.

3. Trace the letters on each word tile. Say the letters. Say the word.

4. Choose a new cereal box. Match more words.

5. Make your own cereal box design. Use some of the words on your word tiles. You can use other words too.

Cereal Box Spellers

the	of	and	a	
to	is	it	for	
on	all	can	an	
more	two	like	make	
very	as	one	new	
only	has	with	from	
that	this	first	each	
you	day	at	be	
do	in	what	from	
over	too	any	ten	
good	will	these	your	

Compound Word Birds

Children pair birds to build compound words—an activity that encourages them to consider word parts when trying to pronounce and figure out the meaning of larger words.

Materials

- shoe box
- box label
- student directions
- scissors
- glue
- game board (page 58)
- bird patterns (page 59)
- resealable plastic bag
- paper
- pencils

Shoe Box Setup

Copy the game board and bird patterns onto card stock. Cut apart the birds and place in a resealable plastic bag. Place the game board, birds, paper, and pencils in the shoe box. Glue the label to one end of the box and the student directions to the inside of the lid.

TIP Make additional sets of compound word birds to play with. Include the words *bird* and *house* in each set, and use the blank bird cards to add new compound words— for example: *bird, house, snow, ball, base, flake, dog, hot, sand, box, paper, news, foot, print, note, book.*

Strengthening Word Analysis Strategies

Compound Word Birds

Directions

(1) Shuffle the bird cards. Place two cards faceup on each birdhouse. Deal the cards from the top.

(2) Help the mixed-up birds find their homes. Move one bird to a new house to spell a compound word. Place the extra bird from the new house in the empty space.

(3) Move another bird to a new home to spell a compound word. If more than one person is playing, take turns moving birds to their homes.

(4) Play until you have paired as many birds as you can. Write the words you make on your paper.

Compound Word Birds

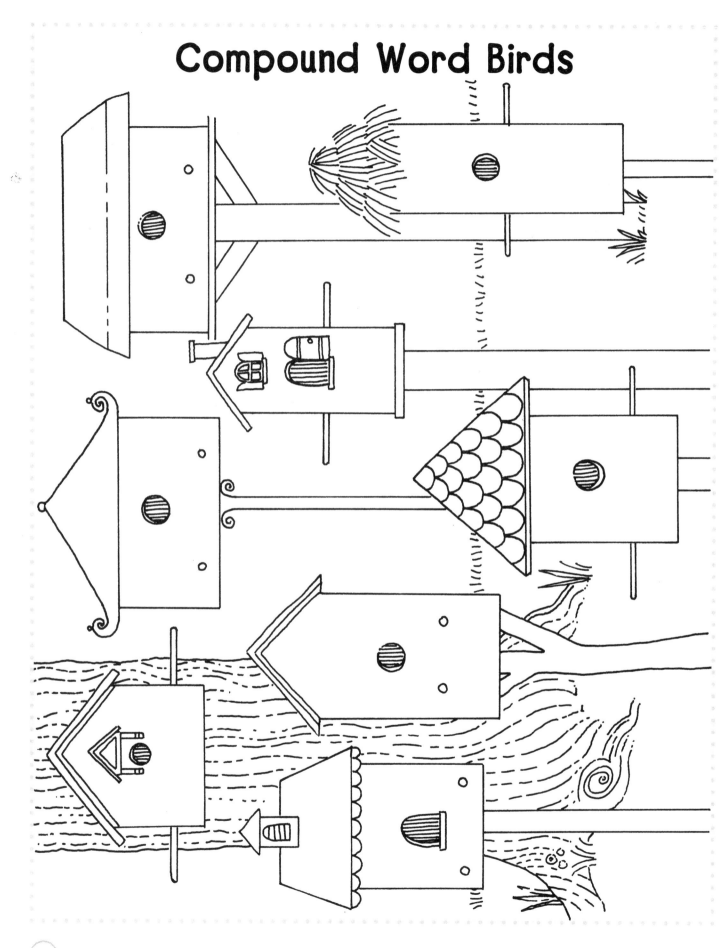

Compound Word Birds

Undo, Redo

Children take apart and put together markers to learn how prefixes change words.

Materials

- shoe box
- box label
- student directions
- scissors
- glue
- dried-up markers
- paper
- pencils
- highlighters

Shoe Box Setup

Collect a dozen or so dried-up markers and remove the inside of each. Write the prefixes *un-* and *re-* on the marker caps (one per cap). Write root words that can be used to form words with these prefixes on the marker bottoms—for example, *do, buckle, tie, bend, clip, cover, fold,* and *pack* (one word per marker). You can also include words that make a new word with one prefix but not the other, such as *happy* and *safe*. Place marker caps and bottoms, paper, pencils, and highlighters in the shoe box. Glue the label to one end of the box and the student directions to the inside of the lid.

TIP To expand this center, add markers with other prefixes, such as *in-, im-, ir-,* and *ill-*. Include new root words as needed so that students can form words.

Learning How Prefixes Change Words

Undo, Redo

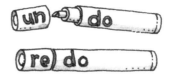

Directions

1 Choose a marker cap and bottom. Put them together. Say the word. Write it on your paper.

2 Undo the marker cap. Place it on a new marker bottom. Say the word. Write it on your paper.

3 Make more words by putting caps on bottoms. Write your words on the paper.

4 Read the words on your list. Highlight the prefix in each.

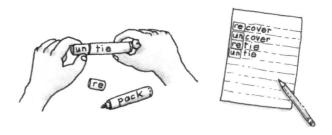

The End!

Children explore root words, meanings, and spelling changes.

Materials

- shoe box
- box label
- student directions
- scissors
- glue
- card templates (page 62)
- pictures (photos or from magazines)
- markers
- large, colorful paper clips

Shoe Box Setup

Copy the card templates onto card stock. Cut apart the cards. Glue a picture that represents a word with a suffix (*-s*, *-er*, *-ing*, or *-ed*) to the left side of each card. Under each picture, write a simple sentence that describes what is happening. Highlight the word with the suffix. Examples follow (words with endings are underlined):

- The <u>frogs</u> hop.
- The girl is <u>walking</u>.
- There are five <u>hats</u>.
- The boy is <u>digging</u>.

For self-checking, write the highlighted word on the back of each card and put a box around the ending. Place the cards and clips in the shoe box. Glue the label to one end of the box and the student directions to the inside of the lid.

TIP As a challenge, include inflectional endings that represent spelling changes. This includes doubling the final consonant (*bigger*, *thinner*) and changing the final *-y* to *-i* (*happier*, *sunnier*).

Identifying Word Endings

The End!

Directions

(1) Choose a card. Tell what is happening in the picture.

(2) Read the sentence. What ending do you hear in the underlined word?

(3) Attach the clip next to the ending that matches.

(4) Look at the back of the card. Check your answer.

Repeat steps 1 through 4 with new cards.

Name _____ Date _____

The End!

s

er

ing

ed

_____

Name _____ Date _____

The End!

s

er

ing

ed

_____

Mystery Box Plurals

Children guess by touch the identity of mystery objects and match the word for the plural form.

Materials

- shoe box
- box label
- student directions
- scissors
- glue
- dark fabric
- collections of small objects (such as toy cars, erasers, beads, and coins)
- brown paper lunch bags
- index cards
- marker

Shoe Box Setup

Cut a wrist-size hole in one end of the shoe box. Tape or glue the fabric to the inside of the box to create a flap that covers the hole. Place each set of objects in a lunch bag. Make word cards that correspond to both the singular and plural form for each object—for example, *car, cars*. Place the bags and word cards in the shoe box. Glue the label to one end of the box and the student directions to the inside of the lid.

TIP Extend students' explorations with plurals by providing a set of picture cards and matching words for both the singular and plural form of each object—for example, *girl, girls; boy, boys; apple, apples*. Have children match words to pictures. For self-checking, write the corresponding word on the back of each picture.

Forming Plurals

Mystery Box Plurals

Directions
(for 2 players)

1 Take all the materials out of the shoe box.

2 Player 1 closes his or her eyes. Player 2 chooses a bag (without looking inside first) and empties the objects into the shoe box.

3 Player 1 puts his or her hand through the hole and feels the objects. This player guesses what's inside the box and finds the word card that matches.

4 Players change places and repeat with a new bag of objects.

Who's Got the Homophone?

Children play a matching game to practice reading and using words that sound the same but have different spellings and meanings.

Materials

- shoe box
- box label
- student directions
- scissors
- glue
- homophone picture and word cards (page 65)
- resealable plastic bags
- paper
- pencils

Shoe Box Setup

Copy, laminate, and cut apart the picture and word cards. Place each set of cards in a resealable plastic bag. To make it easy for children to put this game away, copy the picture cards on one color paper and the word cards on another. Place cards, paper, and pencils in the shoe box. Glue the label to one end of the box and the student directions to the inside of the lid.

TIP To simplify the game, have children deal the word cards equally between players. Players place the cards faceup in front of them. When one child shows and reads a picture card, all players look at their cards to see if they have the match. As with the original version, players use both words in a sentence and keep a list of the words they match.

Recognizing and Using Homophones

Who's Got the Homophone?

Directions
(for 2 or 4 players)

(1) Shuffle the picture cards. Place them facedown in rows. Shuffle the word cards. Place them faceup in rows.

(2) Take turns choosing a picture card. Read the word. Show the picture. Other players try to be the first to find the matching homophone.

(3) The player who finds the matching card uses both words in a sentence. Example: "I filled the whole hole with dirt."

(4) Matching cards are placed to the side. Each player keeps a list of his or her word pairs.

 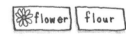

Who's Got the Homophone?

eight	deer	flower
horse	eye	nose
four	knight	one
plane	road	rose
sun	tail	toe
ate	dear	flour
hoarse	I	knows
for	night	won
plain	rode	rows
son	tale	tow

Snapshot Syllable Sort

Children strengthen structural analysis
skills with a sorting game.

Materials

- shoe box
- box label
- student directions
- scissors
- glue
- snapshots of students
- sentence strips
- markers
- record sheets (page 67)
- pencils

Shoe Box Setup

Take snapshots of children (or make
photocopies of existing photographs).
Glue them to sheets of tagboard cut to
create about a 1-inch frame around each
picture. Write each child's name beneath
the photo. On sentence strips, write the
following: one syllable; two syllables; three
syllables; four or more syllables. Make
copies of the record sheets. Place the
photos, sentence strips, record sheets, and
pencils in the shoe box. Glue the label
to one end of the box and the student
directions to the inside of the lid.

TIP If snapshots of students are not
available, you can use pictures
from magazines of animals or
objects. Children name the animal or
object and place it under the correct
sentence strip according to the number
of syllables.

Using Syllabication to Decode Words

Snapshot Syllable Sort

Directions

1 Choose a picture.

2 Read the name. Listen to the number
of syllables. Place the picture under
the sentence strip that tells how many
syllables.

3 Write the name on the record sheet.

4 Repeat steps 1 through 3 with the
other pictures. Which name has the
most syllables? How many syllables do
most classmates' names have?

Name _____

Date _____

Snapshot Syllable Sort

one syllable	two syllables	three syllables	four or more syllables

Name _____

Date _____

Snapshot Syllable Sort

one syllable	two syllables	three syllables	four or more syllables

Bubble, Bubble

Children strengthen structural analysis skills by learning a syllabication rule.

Materials

- shoe box
- box label
- student directions
- scissors
- glue
- game board (page 69)
- word cards (page 70)
- paper clips
- game markers (such as bingo markers)
- 2 pennies (or a number cube with the numbers 1, 2, 3)
- pencils

Shoe Box Setup

Make and laminate a copy of the game board. Make several copies of the word cards and cut them apart. Clip each set of word cards together. Place the game board, cards, game markers, pennies, and pencils in the shoe box. Glue the label to one end of the box and the student directions to the inside of the lid.

TIP Guide children to notice that when two consonants appear in the middle of a word, they can divide the word between them. A good decoding strategy is to try the short-vowel sound for the first part of the word—for example, with the word *bubble*, children might recognize the CVC pattern in the first part of the word (*bub-*) and try the short *-u* sound on this syllable.

Decoding Multisyllabic Words

Bubble, Bubble

Directions
(for 2 players)

1 Place a set of word cards facedown between players. Place a marker on any space. Take turns following steps 2 and 3.

2 Take a card. Then shake and drop the pennies to move: one head, one tail—move 1 space; two heads—move 2 spaces; two tails—move 3 spaces.

3 Use the double letters on the space to try to make a word on the card. If your double letters make a word, write them in the bubbles on the card. If the space says "Free!" you can use any double consonants you want. If the letters do not make a word, place the card at the bottom of the stack. Play until all cards have a word.

Bubble, Bubble

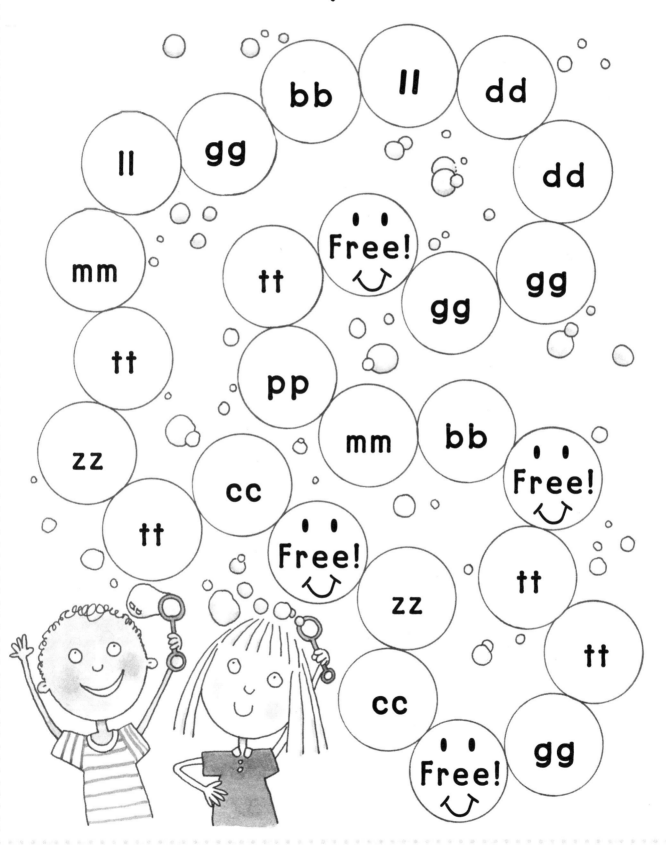

Bubble, Bubble

wi◯◯le	bu◯◯le	su◯◯er
pu◯◯le	mi◯◯le	gi◯◯le
snu◯◯le	bu◯◯er	a◯◯le
ha◯◯er	ra◯◯it	bu◯◯on
le◯◯er	squi◯◯le	so◯◯er
pu◯◯le	ki◯◯en	mi◯◯en

Letter Olympics

Children apply various phonics skills in a set of fun word-building events.

Materials

- shoe box
- box label
- student directions
- scissors
- glue
- letters and trophy pattern (page 72)
- business-size envelopes
- paper
- pencils
- crayons

Shoe Box Setup

Make multiple copies of the letter squares and trophy on card stock. Cut apart each set of letters and place them in an envelope. Place the envelopes, trophies, paper, pencils, and crayons in the shoe box. Glue the label to one end of the box and the student directions to the inside of the lid.

TIP **H**ave children try this activity at different times of the year. Date and save their work so they can see how their results for each event change over time as skills grow. For example, children might find that later in the year, their longest word award goes to an even longer word than it did earlier in the year. For variety and to include different prefixes, suffixes, and so on, make new sets of letters for additional Letter Olympics shoe box centers.

Letter Olympics

Directions

(1) Choose an envelope. Take out the letters.

(2) Choose an event. You can use the same letter more than once to make different words for events 1 and 3.

Event 1: the most words that end in *e*

Event 2: the longest word that begins with *st*

Event 3: the most words that rhyme with *hug*

Event 4: the word with the most syllables

Event 5: the longest word that ends in *s*

(3) For each event, make a trophy for your winning word or words. Write the word or words on the back of the trophy or on a sheet of paper.

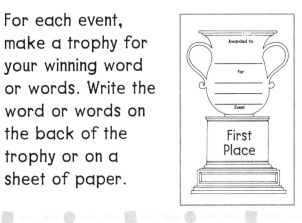

Letter Olympics

s	n	g	i	u	p	d
j	l	r	b	m	c	a
e	i	o	u	g	t	m
n	p	n	w	t	h	e

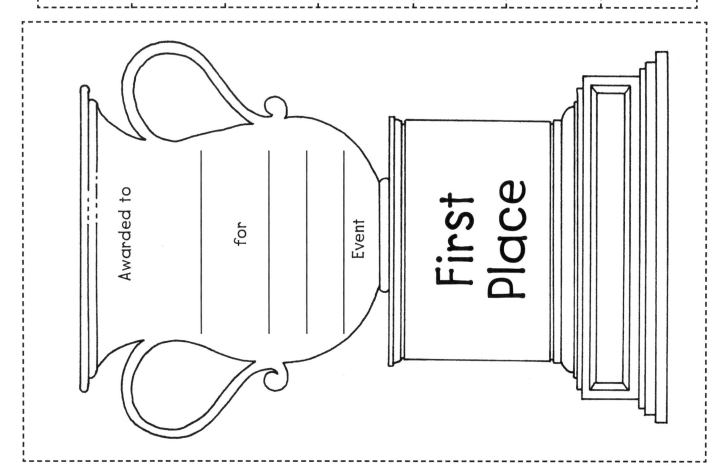

Awarded to

for

Event

First Place

Scoop Shop Spelling

Children use what they know about sound-spelling relationships to make ice cream cones. How many scoops can they add to one cone?

Materials

- shoe box
- box label
- student directions
- scissors
- glue
- ice cream cone and scoop patterns (page 74)
- paper
- pencils

Shoe Box Setup

Copy the ice cream cone and ice cream scoop patterns onto card stock. Make 5 to 10 copies of the ice cream cone and 50 to 100 scoops. Write vowels, vowel digraphs, consonants, consonant clusters, phonograms, endings, prefixes, and suffixes on scoops (one per scoop). Laminate the cones and scoops for durability. Place the cones, scoops, paper, and pencils in the shoe box. Glue the label to one end of the box and the student directions to the inside of the lid.

TIP To simplify this activity, reduce the number of scoops by including only the more basic letter combinations—for example, letters to make CVC words (such as *hum*). Or make three different sets of scoops according to specific skills and place each in a separate bag.

Using Sound-Spelling Relationships to Make Words

Scoop Shop Spelling

Directions

(1) Choose an ice cream cone.

(2) Use the scoops to make words. Can you make a word with two scoops? Can you make a word with more scoops?

(3) Write the words you make on a sheet of paper.

Scoop Shop Spelling

Spot It, Say It, Spell It

This game combines phonics skills with a little daring to see who can build words worth the most points.

Materials

- shoe box
- box label
- student directions
- scissors
- glue
- record sheet (page 76)
- word part cards (pages 77–78)
- resealable plastic bag
- pencils

Shoe Box Setup

Make copies of the record sheet. Copy the word part cards onto card stock. Consider copying each page onto a different-color paper. Cut apart the word part cards and place them in a resealable plastic bag. (The phonograms on page 77 were selected based on the large number of words that can be generated from them. You can add cards to include other phonograms, such as variant vowel phonograms.) Place the record sheets, cards, and pencils in the shoe box. Glue the label to one end of the box and the student directions to the inside of the lid.

TIP To assist players in checking their words, you might make a list of words that can be spelled by putting the cards together in various combinations. Make sure students understand that they may find words that are not on the list. Provide a way to check answers in this case if need be.

Putting Word Parts Together

Spot It, Say It, Spell It

Directions
(for 2 or more players, plus a dealer)

1 The dealer places the cards faceup in a row one at a time.

2 All players look for any two or more cards that spell a word. Example:

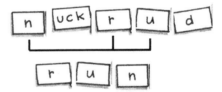

3 When any player makes a word at any time, he or she calls out the word and spells it. If the player is correct, he or she takes the cards and writes the word on the record sheet.

4 The dealer continues to deal cards. Play until players have made as many words as they can. Change dealers. Play again.

Name _____ Date _____

Spot It, Say It, Spell It

two-card word (1 point each)	three-card word (2 points each)	four-card word (3 points each)	five- (or more) card word (10 points each)

- -

Name _____ Date _____

Spot It, Say It, Spell It

two-card word (1 point each)	three-card word (2 points each)	four-card word (3 points each)	five- (or more) card word (10 points each)

Spot It, Say It, Spell It

ack	ail	ain	ake	ale
ame	an	ank	ap	ash
at	ate	aw	ay	eat
ell	est	ice	ick	ide
ight	ill	in	ine	ing
ink	ip	ir	ock	op
oke	ore	or	uck	ug
ump	unk	b	c	d
f	g	h	j	k
l	m	n	p	q

Spot It, Say It, Spell It

r	s	t	v	w
x	y	z	br	cr
dr	fr	gr	pr	tr
sc	sk	sl	sm	sn
sp	st	sw	bl	cl
gl	fl	pl	qu	spr
a	a	e	i	o
u	u	oo	ou	oi
oy	oy	au	s	ing
er	er	ed	y	ly

More Easy-to-Make Shoe Box Learning Centers

Add to your supply of shoe box learning centers and keep student interest strong by rotating in fresh activities. Following are ideas for making more shoe box centers that reinforce phonics skills. For each, use the reproducible templates (right) to make a label and student directions. Glue the label to one end of the box and the student directions to the inside of the lid.

Compound Clip-Ons

With this center, children make and take apart words to build structural analysis skills.

Make word cards that students can put together to form compound words. For example, write the words *after, all, noon, air, mail, plane, sick, any, body, one, thing, where, arm, chair, back, pack, seat, stop, base, ball, basket, bed, time, room, bird, bath, cage, house, birth, day, time, dream, dog, doll, down, hill, stairs, box, book, case, mark, snow, ball, flake, sun, light, rise, burn, sand, pop, corn, field, cob,* and *boat* on cards. Along with the cards, provide clothesline, colorful clips, paper, and pencils. Have children clip cards to the clothesline to build compound words. They can record the words they make, adding to their list each time they use the center.

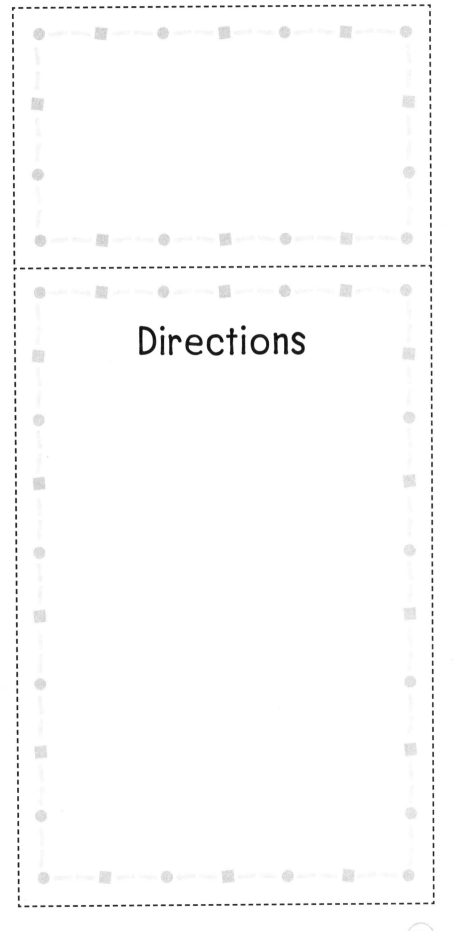

Directions

Spot the Dog

Children practice using what they know about CVC and CCVC spelling patterns to put dots on a dog.

- Draw a large dog. (Or enlarge and trace the one shown here.) Trace it several times on card stock. Cut out the dogs.

- Place a sticky dot on the center of each dog. Write a vowel on each dot. Write consonants and consonant digraphs and clusters on additional dots cut from construction paper. Place the dots in a resealable plastic bag.

- Have children use the dots to form words on the dogs.

- For a fun record sheet, provide a dog to trace, as well as paper and scissors. Children can trace and cut out the dog and record the words they make on it.

Slap and Shout!

This set of word cards provides practice in using structural analysis as a decoding strategy.

Make a set of 20 to 30 word cards with prefixes, suffixes, and root words (one per card). To play, have children shuffle the cards and divide them between two players. Players stack their cards facedown in front of them. On the count of three, players flip over their top card. Players try to make a word by combining the word cards. If the two cards can be used to make a word (such as *un-* and *wind*), the first player to slap the cards and call out the word wins. This player takes the cards and sets them aside. If a player slaps the cards but cannot make a word, the two cards go to the bottom of the player's stack. If neither player can make a word, the cards are set to the side. Play continues until one player is out of cards.

Smiley Face Fun

Reinforce the long *i* vowel sound and final *e* spelling patterns with an activity that lets children stamp smiles on matching words.

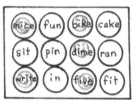

- Draw circles on a sheet of paper. Size them to fit a smiley face stamp. Write a word in each circle. Include some words with a long *i* spelling pattern, such as *bike, mice, dime, kite, five, write, side,* and *might.* Make multiple copies of the word sheet.

- Place the word sheets, a smiley face stamp, and a washable-ink pad in the shoe box.

- To play, have children read the words on the paper, and stamp the ones that have a long *i*, as in *smile.*

- Vary the activity by replacing the smiley face stamp with stamps that represent other vowel sounds or spelling patterns. For example, use fish shapes and a fish stamp for words with a short *i*, snowflake shapes and a snowflake stamp for words with a long *o*, and moon shapes and a moon stamp for words with the vowel digraph *oo.*